ksr Esdn

(26)

THIS PEACE

TRANSLATED FROM THE GERMAN BY

H. T. LOWE-PORTER

THIS PEACE

by

THOMAS MANN

1 9 3 8

NEW YORK

ALFRED A KNOPF

THIS PEACE

THE EVENTS of the past few weeks have plunged a large part of the world — I may still call it the better part — into profound disillusionment, discouragement, and even despair. We have been the shocked, disgusted, and cruelly bewildered spectators at proceedings of far-reaching and decisive significance; it seems vain to hope for any reversal or revision, any possible way in which the outwitted peoples of Europe can come to their senses and see what has been brought to pass in a few days by the swift flow of events. They have too much inherent consistency, those events. They were treachery and crime, in the guise of hypocrisy and demoralized pacifism; but however unfortunate and disastrous, they were too positive, they were rooted too deep in the collective will of Europe, employing as its instrument the classic hypocrisy of English statesmanship, not to be regarded as decisive for many decades to come. Those who had hoped for a better, more humane evolution in Germany and Europe have been as much betrayed, sold out, sacrificed, as the brave little land which stood in the path of German fascism on its march towards European hegemony.

Then must all our previous utterances, all the opinions and strivings which the times had demanded, all the social and political efforts which the past years had laid on the shoulders of myself and others like me — must they all now be thought of as obsolete and valueless, contradicted and refuted by the logic of history? Can they no longer arm the will, but only feed the memory? Or are they perhaps so closely bound up with all that is abidingly true for our Western world, however it may lack actuality for the moment, that they may still serve to keep alive the knowledge of that truth, and herald the dawning of a better time? I do not know. Certainly, so far as my own writings are in

question, they could never have been good reading
for the worshipper of success, for him who cannot
be happy unless he has aligned himself on the side
of the stronger. They can address themselves only
to those whose inmost hearts utter the words: *"Vic-
trix causa diis placuit sed victa Catoni."* In these
words of philosophic resignation the spirit reserves
its right to freedom at the expense of success. It
feels no despair over its defeat in the actual, no
chagrin or remorse, but rather prides itself on having espoused the cause of righteousness even though
it was destined to practical failure at the start. For
surely the task and the rôle of the spirit on this earth
has ever been and will be this very thing. Its pessi-
mism and its magnanimity are equally misunder-
stood by those who suppose that it fights for an ideal
only when it flatters itself that it will soon prove to
be the right one. How have I marvelled, in all these
years, at people who expressed doubts of my attitude towards the political and moral problems of
our time! In naïve inward unconcern they shook
their heads and could not understand "how you
could so uncompromisingly and consistently bet on

the wrong horse." The wrong horse: that means the one that will presumably lose the race; and to "bet on it" seems to such people merely foolish. For them politics is a highly subjective question of shrewdness, of a timely deal with the coming or at latest already arrived power. And not even for any extrinsic advantage; no, simply for "peace of mind" and a need of living in harmony with the known facts. That some people might not care so much about peace of mind as simply and sincerely about their duty to humanity, that is inconceivable to them.

I have in my previous writings borne witness to my knowledge and my all too clear understanding of the mighty movement which we know by the name of fascism. This movement, aided, according to set plan, by the ruling classes of England, won its final triumph in the last days of September 1938. The results of that triumph we are to see far and wide. It was my profoundest, most burning conviction that the movement must be fought, on account of its inherently anti-cultural character — I use the word "cultural" not in a sentimentally æsthetic sense, but rather to express my ideal of humanity and of human dignity. Whatever respect and confidence I had reaped from my artistic work as a creator of human values, I put at the service of the ethical ideals and political forces which seemed most likely to erect a dam against the tidal wave of fascism. I did this while yet in Germany, and afterwards as an émigré. But all the while I really knew that the metaphor should be inverted: in the mind of the masses, it was fascism that was the breakwater which had to hold back the forces of socialism — after exploiting it with all the resources of demagogy at its command. It was against socialism that the hosts of bourgeois Europe were in seething revolt; while I — I continued to see salvation from the cultural disaster of fascist triumph precisely in a voluntary union of the traditionally cultural bourgeoisie and the forces voicing the social demands of the hour.

I did not estimate the fact that Europe was psychologically prepared for the infiltration of fascist ideas into her political, intellectual, and moral life. What I — and not only I — did underestimate was the swiftness of the pace, the decisive influence which fascism would, within a very few years, obtain in the democratic countries. That has been measured for us in the most crushing — and the most infamous — way, by the Czechoslovakian crisis. German émigrés now have this frightful experience in common with those fellow-countrymen still in Germany who shared their desires and hopes: the long-drawn-out torture of the growing realization, repudiated up to the last, that we Germans, inside our country and outside it, were not backed by Europe; that Europe, of which we were a part, from which we expected moral support, did not *in the least desire* the overthrow — several times almost within our grasp — of the National-Socialist dictatorship.

It is hard to make clear to those who have not shared it the martyrdom of this slowly dawning realization. Things were bad enough while they still remained in a negative state. One could understand that the principle of state sovereignty, antiquated though it was, the democratic principle of abstention from interference in the domestic affairs of another country, prevented Europe from taking a hand against proceedings in Germany, however threatening they seemed to the peace and civilization of the Continent. We forced ourselves to understand this; though we — I mean by "we" the German opposition, *extra et intra muros* — could not conceal from ourselves that we felt disillusioned. Here was a state founded on the gangster coup of the Reichstag fire and on the unspeakable quagmire of the trial that followed; a state whose internal policy was plain for all the world to see, while its foreign policy obviously threatened the peace and stability of Europe. How easy it would have been to bring about its diplomatic isolation — at the beginning, or later, say after the purge of June 1934! To make the régime impossible, and to rescue from torture and degradation the Germany whom one professed to love and respect! The Nazis themselves expected intervention. Even in the mildest form it would have sufficed to call a halt.

The intervention never happened. We saw to our amazement that this régime and its unspeakable, often criminal representatives were treated like any other heads of government; that Hitler's pacifistic speeches were gratefully accepted at their face value by a world which seemed to have no notion of the inevitable connexion between home and foreign policy. People *believed* them, or acted as though they did. So long as the Nazis outwardly kept the peace, so long as their chieftain stuck by his assurances that he sought no territorial changes on the Continent, then the world cared not a whit for the fate of the German people, for the atrocities of the concentration camps, the tortures and murders, the persecution of Jews and Christians, the rejection of spirit, the cultural reign of terror, the domination of a philistine bolshevism in the heart of Europe, threatening the very foundations of Occidental civilization.

The return of the Saar to Hitler was much less a matter of course than its return to a German republic. There was a socialist and Catholic opposition, but the powers were careful not to encourage it, and the desired identification of Germany with National-Socialism received the most bewildering confirmation through a plebiscite wherein the victory, though belonging by rights to Germany, was inscribed on the banners of the Nazi party.

It was National-Socialism that reaped the kudos of the naval agreement concluded by England with the Hitler government — independently of France, and in seeming disloyalty to the alliance with her. At least, it seemed so at the time — for nowadays we have learned to doubt whether France was really betrayed, whether indeed the conspiracy of the fascist sympathizers was not even then already maturing.

Hitler's march into the Rhineland happened under the aegis of Great Britain. France might have been tempted to oppose him; but England held her back, though there was not the faintest likelihood of war, since Hitler would have retreated at the first sign of military action on France's part. His generals had in their pockets the order for retreat, to be used in case of need. Considering that the occupation and militarizing of the Rhineland paved the way for the annexation of Austria, it is hard to understand the passive attitude of the democracies. Or, let me correct myself, it would be hard if we did not know their guilty conscience in respect of the Versailles Treaty. That had long since become a dead letter; but penance still had to be done for its territorial provisions. The knowledge of what a German peace might have been, imposed by a victorious Germany in 1918, has never been vivid enough, especially in England, to allay these pangs of conscience. We deemed it a proof of English good faith, good sense, and fair-mindedness that this should be so. Only slowly were our eyes opened to the activities of a set of people who had their corresponding group in France — reactionary, pro-fascist, opposed to the Russian alliance; these exploited the English sense of decency and harnessed it to a policy whose goal was the fascization of the Continent.

Austria fell. This was not the "Anschluss" which had been denied to the Republic, even in its mildest, most purely economic form. It was annexation, conquest. It was accepted by the world in a fatalistic spirit; probably because with the break-up of the old Austrian Empire the union of the German part of it with the Reich had come to seem only a matter of time. But such a view had not obtained in the time of the Republic; it prevailed only after Germany had become once more a military power — with the consent and under the favour of England. And even so, the corrective for such a view was at hand: the Austrians were no German tribe, like the Pomeranians and Saxons, but the integrated product of a specially desirable cultural mixture, with a special cultural and humanizing mission. The denaturing of Vienna — which took place, of course, under the most repellent and infamous circumstances — her degradation into a German provincial town, was a cultural disaster. Inside Germany and out, the old imperial idea was used like a marked card in a gambling game. Austria had never belonged to Germany; you might even say that Germany belonged to Austria.

The annexation took place at a moment when the Nazi dictatorship was in very deep water, economically and in morale. The hopes of the other Germany were in a fair way of fulfilment. Another Abyssinia was a bitter necessity to the régime — and England gave it to them. There was no more room for doubt. England wanted and was working for the preservation and reinforcement of the National-Socialist régime. She vouchsafed it a territorial enlargement which meant, for everybody with eyes in his head, the first step — or, rather, the fourth or fifth — towards the goal. And we learned that France was paralysed not merely by dependence on England and reliance on the entente. We learned it shortly thereafter, when M. Flandin, in an interview, declared that German expansion eastwards was conformable to natural law, and that France must fraternize with the Third Reich. We consoled ourselves with the thought that this was the irresponsible utterance of a reactionary outsider; actually it betrayed the game that was going on, much more unmistakably than we cared to admit to ourselves. Just as unmistakably as did the *Times* editorial, at a later stage, with its gentle suggestion, afterwards officially denied, that the Sudetenland be quite simply ceded to Germany. The editorial even referred to the gain which would accrue to the stout little Czech Republic from this rectification of its borders.

This Peace

At last it was clear — or ought to have been clear — to everybody: there prevailed in the capitalist democracies of the west a sentiment stronger than any antipathy for Nazi Germany's mob rule and gangsterdom, for its debasement of moral standards, its shattering effect on cultural values; a sentiment stronger even than its fear of the anarchistic theory of nationalism, so perilous to the security of all established states. I mean the nightmare of bolshevism, the dread of socialism and of Russia. This it was that brought about the capitulation of democracy as a political and intellectual concept, and drove it to affirm the Hitler thesis, the division of the world into two camps, fascist and communist. This it was that made conservative Europe take refuge behind the fascist bulwark. Nobody would have deemed it possible that what had happened in Germany would repeat itself with such exactness and detail in the rest of Europe. It is uncanny to see how the wretched figure of von Papen, the conservative who delivered up Germany to Hitler, recurs again in the English Chamberlain. Everything is the same: the treachery, the underlying motives, above all the fundamental self-deception — since anyone can see that the forces there invoked to serve the end of any sort of conservatism were themselves a form of bolshevism, on a lower moral plane and without the humanitarian element. Yes, everything was the same — with this difference, perhaps, that Chamberlain had, temporarily at least, more prospect of curbing and taming his unruly protégé after helping him to power — if only he had felt himself responsible for seizing the opportunity! They had given up Austria to the Nazis, good; they were then in a position to impose certain conditions dictated by decency. They did not do it. Probably that would have been regarded as "interference in internal affairs." For everything that befell unhappy Vienna — and the newspaper accounts are a pale reflection of the actual reality — for the unimaginable fate in store for Schuschnigg, who did nothing at all save defend the independence of a country whose human values were entirely foreign to the German Reich, and in so doing had relied on the oft-reiterated sympathy of Europe; for all these horrors England, as the protector of the Nazi invasion, bears the full responsibility. We do not hold beasts and moral defectives responsible for their acts. England, again, bears the shame for the "purge" now being carried out by Henlein's myrmidons in the ceded Sudeten territories, among the Czechs and those Germans who had no desire to be liberated by the Nazis. Here too it would seem to have been possible — one would like to say imperative — to lay down conditions, in order that the programme long since conceded and agreed upon might be carried out with a certain decency. But England magnanimously refrained. Nor was any attempt made to influence the abnormal decisions of the broken and distracted Czech state when, in its new character of fascist appendage to Hitler's empire, it compelled the German emigrants to leave the country within forty-eight hours, without passports, on pain of being delivered up to Germany. It is hard to imagine the mentality of these British statesmen, conscientious only in the service of their own class and their own interests, passing their days in their clubs and their government offices, their week-ends in the country — and wholly undisturbed by thoughts of the thousandfold cases of individual tragedy which were willy-nilly the accompaniment to their astute calculations.

It is one of the foulest pages in history, this story of the betrayal of the Czechoslovak Republic by European democracy; this offering up of an allied and loyal state upon the altar of fascism, that fascism might be preserved and strengthened for its rôle as hired bravo against Russia and socialism. The plot was formed and carried out by a politically powerful clique of international interests, over the heads of the people, whose hearts are full to over-flowing with gratitude that "war was averted," but whose eyes have not yet been opened to the way in which they have been betrayed. It was a monstrous abuse, a cruel practical joke played on their nerves and heart-strings and their justified and universal fear of war — a war which was never intended, which, despite all the gas-masks, black-outs, and trenches, never seriously threatened. And when I say "the people," I include all of us; we have all been hoaxed and befooled, driven wantonly to and fro between hope and despair, been made the pawns in a shameless game.

The fault is ours — though perhaps it is to our credit that we were not politicians enough to see through it. Despite all that had gone before, including the transparently disingenuous and disgraceful comedy of non-intervention, carried out by England in favour of Franco, we could not credit the possibility of such heaped-up knavery and manœuvring. Our simplicity was culpable. What else could it be but hypocrisy, to behave as though one believed in those pulings about "our brothers in Sudetenland," when everybody knew that it was not a question of the brothers, but of the Skoda works, Czech industry, Rumanian oil, Hungarian grain, Germany's economic penetration eastwards, the liquidation of Czechoslovakia as a military and diplomatic factor, the break-up of the French and Russian alliance, the isolation of France? Our distress mounted intolerably, through the Runciman mission's days and weeks of palavering, the slow attrition of the Czechs as more and more impossible concessions were exacted from them; all that sank deeper and deeper into our consciousness, yet we never went quite far enough; never did the simple, shameful truth quite dawn upon us that the surrender to Hitler of the Republic of Masaryk had been for a long time a settled fact.

Yet that was the truth. And today the successful gambler of Berchtesgaden can glory in the triumph he has, "without bloodshed," without drawing the sword, brought home to the German people; that is, to the Nazi party; such a tremendous and decisive triumph that he can boast of having fundamentally shifted the balance of power in Europe and in a space of five years repeated on a continental scale his rise to power in 1933. But, we may well ask, when did the fellow realize that everything was possible save only open military onslaught upon the obstacle in his path? That was forbidden — because in that case France was formally and juridically bound to come to the rescue. But everything else he wanted he might have. When did he realize it? Probably later than the rest of us; for it seems that the warnings of Göring and Mussolini were necessary to prevent him, in the last days of September, from stumbling blindly to destruction, into a war which nobody expected of him and a defeat from which everybody tenderly tried to protect him.

It is laughable to see how this great man has been kept in leading-strings by the skill of the pro-fascist English statesmen. Convinced, and rightly, of England's goodwill, he thought in May that he could simply overrun Czechoslovakia. He was prevented from doing this; to his great amazement and wrath, for he did not see the good intentions behind the act. That was no way of doing things: he might thus clumsily invoke the *casus foederis*, for to leave Czechoslovakia in the lurch when she was directly attacked would have put too great a strain on international ethics and too flagrantly compromised the loyalty of the democracies to their alliances. Treachery was indicated; but in the case of a war caused by unprovoked aggression, in the most literal sense of the words, decency forbade it. There are, however, other, less explicit forms of attack and betrayal, which permit one to save one's face. The trick had to be turned, Europe had to be put in the pot — but it would take time. They say that the

Führer's genius lies in his knowing how to bide his
time. But he did not want to bide his time. His
English governess had her hands full to make him.
The summer passed in grooming the delicate situation; then things had got on far enough so that it
could come out into the open; and the nations were
prevented with a trumped-up alternative: Czechoslovakia must be sacrificed, or the world would be
plunged into the horrors of war.

It was an ignoble trick. The peoples' fear of war
and yearning for peace were exploited, just as their
guilty conscience in respect of Versailles had been
exploited before. They were deliberately terrorized,
their hopes and fears were played upon from hour
to hour. The alternative of war or peace never
existed. Never was it necessary to save peace by
means of treachery, by yielding to dishonour, and
by making of France a nation defeated and in-
capable of alliances. Peace was to be had, quite
simply and in complete security, only if the western
states, certain of the moral support of America, had
stood shoulder to shoulder with Russia for the pro-
tection of Czechoslovakia. And indeed there was a

moment when it looked as though there might be an international popular movement which would force the corrupt governments to seek that honourable kind of peace. I shall never forget the roar of applause from twenty thousand throats which greeted my words, in Madison Square Garden on September 26: "It is too late for the British government to save the peace. They have lost too many opportunities. Now it is the peoples' turn. Hitler must fall! That alone can preserve the peace!"

He would have fallen. The dream of the last five years was within a hair's breadth of fulfilment. Germany might have been driven, not into war, but up to the verge of it; and Germany and the world might have been freed overnight from the incubus of Nazi tyranny. Italy had revoked. That was to be expected. Never for a moment did I think that Italy, even a fascist Italy, would fight on Germany's side against Europe. In my letter to the Dean of the Philosophical Faculty of the University of Bonn I had said that Germany, at the decisive moment, would stand alone. She was already alone. Mussolini could never have brought Italy into such a war.

He would have been overthrown, and his German boon companion would have followed him. The hero of Germany could neither advance nor retreat. Either would have spelled his undoing. He might possibly, none the less, have tried to hurl himself and "his" nation into a war foredoomed to failure; but it would never even have broken out — before things got that far, the war-maker would have been removed by the people and the army. The very revelation that his mission had been nothing more or less than to lead Germany into a suicidal war with the whole world, the revelation of the truth that this régime had from the beginning borne the seed of collapse within itself — that would have been enough to prove its bankruptcy. Hope made us tremble. Not yet six years of it, and now this loathsome spectre was to vanish, the horrid vision of a National-Socialist millennium would be no more. It had come much sooner than we had dared to hope, but we had always known that it was bound to come. Twenty-four hours of firm resolve on the part of the mild-mannered democracies whose compliance had so maddened us, and the author of all our sufferings, the corrupter of Europe, would have played out his hand; European fascism would be physically, mentally, morally finished; and the way would be open for a new social humanism, upon which the best minds of the age were everywhere at work; for the return of the genius of peace, of labour, and of human dignity.

It was not to be. For the collapse of fascism was precisely what the governing classes of England did not want. They had never wanted it. They did not want war, because they did not want a common triumph with Russia, or the collapse of fascism — a war that would have been over almost before it had begun. And for this, for such a kind of peace, they have been hailed as deliverers by the agonized peoples of Europe. For twenty-four hours the *par nobile fratrum* of Rome and Berlin were in a desperate situation. England rescued them. A few hints to the effect that "violence was out of the question," but that everything could be put straight in a short conversation; that was enough to bring about the eleventh-hour conference in Munich. The prophecy in my letter, that "war will not be permitted" to

Germany — that came true; but she was prevented in a strangely considerate way. Hitler was not "permitted" to bring about the ruin of fascism. Without recourse to "violence" he got everything which he might have ruined himself to get by violence. Amid the jubilations of the victimized populations, shedding tears of joy and relief, Bohemia was returned to an empire to which it never belonged; Czech districts "with more than fifty per cent of German inhabitants" were delivered up to German domination, along with German-speaking democrats, socialists, and Jews, whose lot would now certainly be a tragic one. Without pity, without a thought for the thousandfold tragedy of human suffering or for the agony of a courageous people which had been ready to fight for its freedom and for the sake of freedom as an ideal; unmoved by the fate of Germany itself, and the mental and spiritual future of its citizens; this immense triumph was granted to the Gestapo government, a triumph which secured its position for a long time to come. The Czech government, the eastern bulwark of democracy, was destroyed or deliberately converted into a broken-spirited dependency of National-Socialism. The Continental hegemony of Hitler-Germany was signed and sealed, Europe was sold into slavery. And the reimbursement for all that? It was this peace.

We have been told that the Peace of 1918 could not endure, because it was based on the unconscionable Treaty of Versailles. By the same moral standards we may judge that no good can come of a peace founded like this one, on the vilest of treachery and betrayal of the peoples. Are the nations now disarming? Does Germany in particular make the smallest movement toward dissolving its concentration camps, ceasing its religious and racial persecutions, or conforming to civilized standards? It does not occur to it; perhaps to its people, but not to its government. For the régime would then be superfluous, it would prepare its own surrender, the moment it stopped gesturing and posturing and indulging in the heroics which are its lifeblood. But there can be no peace in Europe so long as a great people in its midst pursues a policy of spiritual and moral desolation.

There are those, in England and elsewhere, who consider that the peace is but a truce and that war must come before long. They are quite right — even though they do not have to be right in the end. For one may be right a thousand times in the name of all reason and morality, and yet not need to be right in the end. Have we not learned this, after all these years? Is not that at once our everlasting shame and our abiding consolation? It is hard to comprehend why those who did not want war, when it would scarcely have had to be waged, should wish or be forced to wage it under conditions of far greater difficulty. Obviously, we have come to a point where war is to be avoided at all costs. Armaments are no longer accumulated to wage war, but only to levy blackmail and to counter it. If the western powers now, after their capitulation, increase their armaments, one is justified in the supposition that they wish to be able to deal with blackmail more successfully in the future.

The crisis — or rather the pretended crisis, for there was never an idea of fighting — has achieved two things: first, the bad conscience of the democra-

This Peace

cies over the peace of Versailles is finally appeased. They have undone, down to the very last shred, their victory of 1918; they have recognized it as a historical error, and step by step they have retreated before Germany. It is a sight unprecedented in history. By a combined policy of non-resistance they have put Germany where she would have been if she had been victorious in 1914; more they cannot do to atone for the blunders and stupidities of the peace. Their souls are free from guilt, they have no more penances to perform; and that may weigh in the position they take up towards future threats and demands.

And secondly, these last days of September showed that the people of Germany suffered from a dread of war no whit less acute than that felt in other countries. All the heroic methods and discipline of the past six years proved, when the test came, to have borne no fruit. The extravagant joy and thankfulness with which Germany, too, greeted the peace would, I venture to say, have been just as great if it had brought no territorial aggrandizement with it. It merely bore witness to the anguish of fear out of which it sprang, and it was a proof of the unpopularity of dynamic politics. Here too we may see a hopeful sign for the future.

We may add a third consolation to these two. The Continent will now rapidly become fascist — that is the deliberate issue of the English policy. But we need not consider this entirely on its negative side, as the triumph of a hated antagonist. It is at once a counter-measure and a kind of adaptation, taking cognizance of the need to counterbalance the unfair advantages of the other side and put oneself on a more equal footing. It would involve considerable sacrifices, moral and spiritual; sacrifices of freedom, civilization, and human dignity. Yet it would not be only a descent, but also a method of defence. Who can guess the riddle of destiny? The triumph of fascism might perhaps end in self-destruction. A continent of people all shaven and shorn fascist-fashion might, by the irony of fate and urged by economic considerations, become a United States of Europe. And then? The trashy ideology which served as vehicle on the road to such a goal might have become superfluous, or even useless, and more humane conceptions would again obtain a hearing in the sphere of Occidental culture. For just as fascism excludes peace, so peace excludes fascism.

Madness, thou hast prevailed. . . . But we need not therefore think that we must sink altogether. Reason and spirit have known, through many thousand years, that things do not go their way on this earth; surely they have not been confuted, or crushed, or given the lie, by a defeat as preposterous as this. It is the way of the world — it always has been; but that does not mean we did wrong to wish it otherwise. To be against such a thing as Hitler is always to be right, let it turn out as it will. The way that history has taken in this instance is so foul, it has such a stench of lying and knavery, that no man need be ashamed of having refused to take it. And who can say whether it will not still lead through such abominations that we are justified of our faith?

We must have no fear. Reason and truth may suffer apparent eclipse. But in us, in our hearts, they are eternally free. And looking down from the bright regions of art, the spirit may laugh at the triumphant folly of the hour. Not forsaken and alone, but secure in the bond uniting it with all that is best on earth.

American Editions of the Works of

THOMAS MANN

ROYAL HIGHNESS. *Translated by* A. Cecil Curtis. 1916.
(out of print)

BUDDENBROOKS. *Translated by* H. T. Lowe-Porter. 1924

DEATH IN VENICE AND OTHER STORIES.* *Translated by*
Kenneth Burke. 1925

THE MAGIC MOUNTAIN. *Translated by* H. T. Lowe-Porter.
1927

CHILDREN AND FOOLS.* *Translated by* Herman George
Scheffauer. 1928

THREE ESSAYS. *Translated by* H. T. Lowe-Porter. 1929

EARLY SORROW.* *Translated by* Herman George Scheffauer. 1930

A MAN AND HIS DOG.* *Translated by* Herman George
Scheffauer. 1930

DEATH IN VENICE.** *A new translation by* H. T. Lowe-
Porter, *with an Introduction by* Ludwig Lewisohn.
1930

MARIO AND THE MAGICIAN.** *Translated by* H. T. Lowe-
Porter. 1931

* These stories are now included, in translations by Mrs. Lowe-
Porter, in *Stories of Three Decades.*
** Now included in *Stories of Three Decades.*

Bibliography

PAST MASTERS AND OTHER PAPERS. *Translated by* H. T. Lowe-Porter. 1933. (out of print)

JOSEPH AND HIS BROTHERS. *I. Joseph and His Brothers. 1934. II. Young Joseph. 1935. III (two volumes). Joseph in Egypt. 1938. Translated by* H. T. Lowe-Porter

STORIES OF THREE DECADES. *Translated by* H. T. Lowe-Porter. 1936

AN EXCHANGE OF LETTERS. *Translated by* H. T. Lowe-Porter. 1937

FREUD, GOETHE, WAGNER. *Translated by* H. T. Lowe-Porter and Rita Matthias-Reil. 1937

THE COMING VICTORY OF DEMOCRACY. *Translated by* Agnes E. Meyer. 1938